STAR POWER

STAR POWER

SERAPHINA WILDE

CONTENTS

CHAPTER 1

Introduction

Celebrity culture dominates much of today's media, but many of the celebrities we know and love are not quite the same as the stars of the past. Footballers from the Premier League, pop singers, and royals from around the world now make up the vast majority of the names that we see splashed across the tabloid headlines. We love stars – people that are put up on a pedestal to shine with a superhuman glow. We delight in their victories and egotistically smirk at their failures. Further to this, we also aspire to be just like them, imitating their hairstyle, clothing, or accent, and idolizing those that model behaviors we find compelling. From the Greek hero of mythology, the god-like superstar of the interwar screen, to modern folkloric Spiderman, pop sensations, and mega-rich reality TV stars, celebrities capture our imagination and star in the story of our global creative imagination.

People all over the world are infatuated with celebrities. The celebrity industry in some countries has gone so far as eclipsing all other forms of cultural production to become a premier source of meaning and morals. We look to celebrities as the modern paragons of virtue, the people to emulate. For better or for worse, there is no denying that iconic people are not just 'people' anymore. They are much more than that. That hardly any field is not carpeted with the characteristics of celebrity illustrates quite a remarkable turn in the latter day of secular society. There is a whole host of literature, theory, and research on celebrity in sociology. Celebrity has also been questioned from a moral view as what on earth causes anyone to think that they are 1) different from others in some way that in the morally proper way confers entitlement and 2) confers appropriate judgment of the others? For example, Karen Kleege offers a variety of lucid and challenging critiques of the theory of celebrity. A large portion of this literature, though, looks at very particular celebrities who are most often folk devils, such as criminal celebrities. The study of the grand and positive superstar has been relatively unexplored. To many, they hold the aura and mystique of world-reaching yet personal deities.

Background and Significance
Celebrity culture represents a pervasive aspect of contemporary society, helping to shape diverse domains like economics, law, politics, and culture. People often regard celebrities as stunningly powerful and important: single human beings who appear to be bigger than life itself. However, it has not always been like this, and scholars have striven to understand celebrity's grand importance. There are many components to the celebrity phenomenon, and, as is true for all elements that shape human society, this event has emerged and changed due to a variety of interweaving forces and conditions. The historical record provides valuable context for the reverberating historic, social, and cultural impact of celebrity, but the record can also be elusive and ambiguous, replete with factual inaccuracies.

Scholars have broadened definitions of what it means to be a "celebrity," moving away from characterizing celebrity as a purely modern invention or confining fame to any one culture or period. suggest that celebrities are interesting not only as individuals, but also as signs. Stars are essentially products of the entertainment industry, manufactured and manipulated to exemplify mass culture values which they in turn reflect. They represent archetype situations, themes, characters, and actions, and are often used for motivational purposes in addition to simply entertainment. These people often do not hold special degrees or permits, nor are they politicians or other representative heirs. They come from a variety of places and backgrounds, and they are not elected or selected.

Purpose and Scope

The aim of this essay is to investigate the influences and impact of celebrity icons in contemporary popular culture and local social networks. The purposes of this study are exploratory, and to offer an insight into three aspects of the subject: neoteny and ageless youth, near-superhuman status and the construction of celebrity skill, and digital folk psychology and fascinations of celebrity ordinary. Informing the overall qualitative research ambitions of mine, the essay is the first part in a larger series of studies using focus groups and dyadic interviews to investigate celebrity influence operating in sociocultural borders around the small-scale worlds of two rural towns in North East England.

All who participated could be said to live in a global world of celebrity, but one that may only lightly touch upon the subject matter as loosely connected to the cultural landscapes of rural life and lifestylisms. Methodologically speaking, focus groups and interviews have been chosen because of a deficit of direct empirical insight. Earlier studies have tended to be quantitative and are based around the Western, English-speaking individual in America, England, New Zealand or Australia. The scale of such research aims to identify the likelihood of things relying on particular positions held by those who are asked. Findings offer a potential picture of the nature of a 'dispositional to identify' person as they exist or respond in some coherent way as cultures and occasionally cultural interpretations, but they say little about how celebrity operates unnoticed within lived experience.

CHAPTER 2

The Evolution of Celebrity Culture

Celebrity characters have always populated human culture and history, smiling down at us from pages of the past or twinkling back at us from screens. Over time, the stories of celebrities have evolved from being pure myth, current affairs, historical figures, Roman Emperors, Kings, politicians, stage actors, film stars, soap stars, reality TV stars, models, public figures, influencers, and people of greater infamy like mass murderers. "Celebrity" as we perceive it now has a rather defined history, becoming what it is today largely post-World War II and being invented as we see it today in Hopper & Hopper's pioneering work on the subject, 2006's "Telling Lives: The Biographer's Art."

It is largely perceived that with the invention of cinema, celebrities with the capital C as we know them today grew. They were first Hollywood movie stars and, in fact, the first "modern" celebrities. Heroes of war, magicians, aviators, and even gangsters and politicians all received the same tabloid press coverage. Post-World War II and in times of peace, the media began focusing more and more on the celebrities. In the 1950s, people's values became somewhat retrospective, and movie stars and musicians from the past became a hot topic of the previously mentioned "youngsters press." Frank Sinatra, Liza Minnelli, Judy Garland, and Mick Jagger were all a big deal once again. Unlike Hollywood's royalty we have today, this time around, there was much more focus on the star's personal life and their off-screen triumphs and tragedies. Before cinema, we had a few notable stars; impresario Mae Celeste, Lord Byron, and American painter Gilbert Stuart fluttered in and out of the spotlight and court circulars of their time.

Historical Overview

Historical Overview: The notion of the celebrity has become a dominant issue for the last century. In the 17th year, the first discovery of value in "real life" allowed the dim lines between those that were famous in fact and those of fiction to begin to solidify. It was the face of Alexis Clairax who adorned business advertising for the Pears soap that solidified the acceptance that people would be interested in learning not just about stories but real individuals. It was the celebrity that had the power to refashion themselves to satisfy the demands of the public. The celebrity of Lord Byron would forever change the nature of popular culture by inspiring audiences of "The Bride of Abydos" to "fight...bake...draw...[and] make a fuss" and inspired artists after his own death to begin using their art to engage the public in the discussion on what is "real" life—or at least what is real in the reckoning of the artist. This section will take time to help readers see the journey from Alexander the Great to LeBron James as contextualizing the creation and consumption of popular culture figures.

Gone are the days that celebrities were both believed in and yet knowingly confected. From this point on, Byron's passion, his tempestuousness, was to become less significant in the popular imagination than his celebrity. In an afterword titled "Survival of the

Fittest," intelligent designer best classified individuals via sociopath, personality-disorder rating. Going further, the distinction between celebrity, has-been, and wannabe came with Nikes having Aureal to dollars in sales when sold at approximately the same time in 2004. Beginning in the 1930s, the first scientific publication, Journal of Social Psychology, began publishing articles with "celebrity" as part and parcel of the research within.

Technological Advancements and Social Media

In addition to the star system and its perks of reward, modern technology and social media have played a significant impact in the increased visibility of today's stars. Since the 1980s, the star system has been modified from simply a promotional vehicle to that of a solid, marketable commodity. New media has continued to shape this transformation, providing stars unparalleled outlets to present their brand. As De Certeau writes, "camera, printing, and the phonograph changed the relation between the living present and its past, giving memory in the form of images and sonorous traces a status other than that of monument. By reappropriating the irreversibility into which every lived moment is embraced (like the return of the dead in their new bodies that are more marvelous and immortal than ever), these apparatuses outline the horizon of a present which becomes the exercise of reproducing, discovering, and replaying the past."

The addition of new technologies can amplify and replicate these meanings, thus serving to further heighten the appeal of such stars. As such, the devotion of so many pages to celebrity culture, whether in gossip magazines, tabloids, or even legitimate news outlets, is a significant development in the history of the star system and its presentation. The emphasis is nowadays not so much on the talents of our celebrities, but rather on the stars as people. They are studies in self-creation-by-proxy, as played out on a very grand scale. To witness the launching of Madonna's latest album, teens waited in queues for up to ten hours in the Southern California heat last month. Given the enormous profits the star system generally brings, the modern technology which made all of this possible can be expected to expand upon the encyclopedia with future volumes.

CHAPTER 3

Psychological and Sociological Perspectives

Outlook

Celebrity worship syndrome can cause distress to functions of an obsessive-compulsive nature. They feel they directly or indirectly represent intimate relationships and friendships with a 'celebrity cum member'. A paper published by the British Journal of Psychology in 2005 stated the functions that are as follows: an essential role in personal identity and self-cultivation are shaped by the obsession and worship of celebrities; several studies have come to refute the notion of self-cultivation and personal identity in a number of studies.

Furthermore, celebrity consumption and admiration are thought to have the power to seduce and prove credibility by way of overwhelming emphasis on the idol. The social comparison theory is based on the assumption that people have a 'natural' tendency to evaluate themselves in terms of other people. Through such affiliative relationships with media stars, viewers are able to express their own - in case of belonging, positive feelings by means of vicarious participation in the exploits of media stars. At another level, parasocial interaction may be used as a means of fulfilling needs for knowledge, using media star exemplars as models for behaviors and choices through which individuals can achieve increased success and satisfaction. Whether expressively tied, capitally rooted in narcissism or egoism; aims to attain happiness, fulfillment, and belongingness by creating and sustaining affiliative relationships with media personalities are intricately associated with the human condition.

Celebrity Worship Syndrome

Celebrity Worship Syndrome, or CWS, refers to the propensity of certain individuals to obsess over and idolize the lives of a celebrity or group of celebrities. The study of CWS has unveiled short- and long-term consequences for those who possess hyper-passion for celebrities as well as for society. Behaviorally, those with CWS have been found to mimic behavior they believe to be characteristic of the celebrity they idolize. Attitudinally, these beliefs about the object of worship tend to take on a rigidity, such that the believers have trouble viewing the celebrity under any light other than a positive one. This glass-half-full perspective implies that the worshippers are not as focused on the potential negatives of the celebrities they worship. And indeed, some work has found that those who worship celebrities were less likely to be critical of them when one of their idols was shown engaging in proscribed behavior such as smoking or drinking.

One potential limitation of these studies is that they tend to focus on college-age women. Critics argue that celebrity worship seemingly is not influencing so-called normal consumers. There are, of course, exceptions to every rule and certainly not every individual will act out in such ways, but there seems to be something fundamentally different about the celebration of Princess Di's life versus the angst many people feel over the untimely passing of a celebrity. Society as a whole does concern itself with what it perceives as senseless loss. Our culture forces us to grieve when we view someone as having maintained near deity status, be it a Princess or any one of many celebrities. This also suggests that the long-range implications of such behavior are less likely simply individual psychopathology and more a function of the cult of celebrity worship in our culture.

Social Comparison Theory

Social comparison theory postulates that people routinely compare themselves with individuals around them, both similar and dissimilar others, in order to learn more about themselves. The theory is based on the fundamental assumption that humans have a basic need to know the truth about themselves. To the extent that a person lacks clear, internal standards with which to judge their abilities, attitudes, and beliefs, they look to the physical and social world, and to the people in it, to generate insight and knowledge about themselves. This principle has a number of implications for the role of the celebrity in society. Practically speaking, people do not always have direct access to others as sources of information, so they look to media sources, marketing, and advertising to provide information about the opinions, beliefs, and norms of cultural icons.

Although people compare themselves to those around them for self-evaluation purposes, members of society can also use this information to establish social norms. Research in social comparison reveals some relevant insights here. First, it has been found that people conform to the opinion of the majority. Asch demonstrated strong conforming behavior in participants when they had to give judgments about visual figures. Normative influence has also been found to work on a personal level, where participants take the opinion of another individual as the appropriate norm. Cialdini illustrated this in a study, whereby he showed how people reduced energy consumption by 20-30 percent simply by being told that the majority of their neighborhood was already doing so.

CHAPTER 4

Economic Implications

Celebrities can be very influential when it comes to convincing consumers to try a specific product or service. This is an effective technique for advertisers because people are prone to react to endorsements based on the reputation or fame of a celebrity, rather than on the products themselves. At the other end of the spectrum, this section also explores the negative impact that may result from an association with a tarnished or controversial celebrity. During the Golden Age of Hollywood in the 1930s, actor Clark Gable endorsed Chesterfield Cigarettes in various print ads.

Branding is a very important factor for companies, and many companies invest a lot of money to develop a celebrity partnership that can assist in creating brand equity. Jennifer Lopez, Britney Spears, and many other celebrities are considered "iconic" by many people. Most of these entertainers have their name attached to a variety of items, including perfume and clothing. The first star to actually venture into this field was Elizabeth Taylor, with a few of her various perfumes. Perfume was her initial merchandise, then she created "the White Diamonds" and her entire clothing line called "House of Taylor." The price of her merchandise alone is absolutely outrageous, especially for a bottle of her perfume. Most of the profits are said to be going to her charities instead of herself. Just recently, Regis Philbin released his line of men's clothing.

Celebrity Endorsements

Despite a long list of factors, when it comes to impacting the advertising market, individuals who have currently or previously been famous, the so-called "celebrities" or "stars," can attract a unique interest of those doing personal marketing. After all, occasionally the only attractive aspect of the product is that it is also associated with the celebrity. If we were to put this in a straightforward, logical manner, a high dissemination degree and a positive public image are the main things that contain value for consumers of this type. The opinions and attitudes of celebrities here serve as proof of the high level of satisfaction of those who regularly perform the role of true "rock stars" or other stars somewhere above the vital goals of the ordinary.

The present study is a survey of stars on supporting advertisements. These are the ones who are known all over their home countries or all over the world and have been waiting for more exposure than most of their compatriots working in various fields. A particular emphasis can be used in a big competition advertisement, commercials, a marketing program, an advertising campaign which is a huge one, etc. It differs from other research in that it records the actual premiums of Hollywood stars for endorsing advertising. This research investigates the economic effect of celebrity endorsement and the identification of famous endorsers.

In recent years, marketers in various product classes like products, drinks, interpersonal networks, articles in the water, and others have used the attractiveness of the celebrity's target consumer by this purpose in a progressive manner. The study of celebrity endorsement is a new effort and a research attempt to assess the impact of star potential. A large number of attempts are also directed at studying the characteristics of famous endorsers that make them effective at attitude, the effectiveness of agreements for celebrity recommendation, and demographics and recommendations for celebrity endorsement. Accurate modeling of the impact of endorsement in personal recommendations from the consumer of the endorser is required for certain outcomes. Furthermore, the potential added-value comes in the moment in the endorsement agreement. To date, in literature, there have not been any tryouts to do this.

Branding and Merchandising

This chapter addresses the issue of branding and merchandising using the examples of celebrities. Many contemporary consumer goods are not commodities in a simple sense, or at least not merely. They instead must be viewed as complex commodity/celebrity/everyday-object hybrids with celebrity and fame acting as hyper-additives to the product's market value. Commodity culture is detrimental to distinctiveness of individuals because it validates mass marketing and manipulates consumer preference of products and celebrities. The concept and phenomena of marketing transcend the basic commercial exchange factors of the historical free market into advertisement and staffing marketing that sells products, promising satisfaction and the allure of a dream. The glorification of commodities means that a housewife that adores an all-purpose tool, a factory girl that adulates a movie star, and both are consumers of a pipedream or Hollywood ideal or carving set of tools that cater to their everyday needs.

Secondly, this concept of merchandising, which sociology qualifies as a social control and consumer studies qualify as demand forecasting, deals with the management of the domestic economy comparative with innovation and technical development. Celebrity branding and advertising provide interesting case studies to understand not only the value creators but also how agency work is valued. Marketers and advertisers often turn to celebrities in order to inspire or encourage public interest in a political issue or cause, to promote a public service message, to integrate them within the parameters of another political or market economy, to serve as a functionally additive to another product or part of a promotional package, or to be the celebrity cred in their own advertisements. This chapter focuses directly on the last option through an exploration of icons, product endorsements of the world's biggest pop entities. Icons like this, representing children's collective sense of "cool," shape children's musical taste, hairstyle, clothes, and also represent 100 million dollar industries.

CHAPTER 5

Political Influence

Actors and actresses, former athletes, authors, singers, and fashion models are often found using their voices to raise awareness and bring attention to political causes. Currently, more than ten United Nations (UN) organizations and four major international non-governmental organizations have begun using celebrities and entertainment personalities to lobby on humanitarian and social development issues. Most of these celebrities take on positions at these organizations as Messengers of Peace, Goodwill Ambassadors, Humanitarian Ambassadors, or National Ambassadors. By having these celebrities represent these organizations, the UN and other non-governmental organizations hope the use of popular culture will reach and unite the peoples of the world around important and vital global issues. Historically, celebrities have provided assistance in gathering attention for specific situations. Over time, many of these citizens of countries visited have lost sight of the overall purpose of having celebrities visit. Many have become numb to the celebrities' persuasion and simply want to see them because they are famous people visiting their country or giving them a hug.

It is a primary assumption behind the selection of these celebrities that their influence could be beneficial since they have the potential to shape conversations about urgent humanitarian and environmental challenges, as well as the ability to reach millions of people and produce significant changes for the better. It is important to note, however, that there are significant risks associated with deploying celebrities. This section looks into the ways in which celebrities influence politics, the effects of celebrities' political influence, and the unintended consequences of using celebrities in these roles.

Celebrity Activism

The term "celebrity activists" can convey the unrealistic image of activism through the influencers (also celebrities and other media channels of communication). This branding strategy of the term is optimistic. A celebrity's voice is powerful in drawing attention to social and political problems, even though they may not be experts in the fields. Celebrities' participation in social and political debates can help publicize issues. They can promote good causes and generate funding for charity. Research has found that celebrity support can lead to more news coverage and social media engagement. Now it is considered ethical for celebrities to give causes a platform and make their voice heard. Ethical appeals have much more potential to succeed.

Although having a heard voice of sharing ideas is essential, bringing a cause a long-lasting impact has to be based on rights and responsibilities. However, in the process of taking on a controversial issue, it is essential to understand and address any objections to your activism. The ethics of celebrity activism revolve around the responsibilities that public figures have when it comes to speaking out on what they perceive to be wrong. For some critics, celebrity activism is controversial, involving pseudo-enlightenment, ideological merchandising, or vanity and celebrities' own interests and power over the public. Critics are suspicious about celebrities' involvement with third world problems. Celebrity today has become a business in itself. Celebrities' careers are predicated on their public image and charitableness is part of this public image.

Celebrity Diplomacy

Being televised before U.S. Congressional committees, unhindered from censorship by the People's Republic of China, or otherwise working on behalf of the Chinese government, witnessed in facilitating channels of communication, showing themselves to the People's Republic as friendly, sensitive, and well-informed agents; Hollywood celebrities and the People's Republic of China seeking to enhance their cooperative associations, allowed some celebrity icons to operate as a sort of intermediary not only between Hollywood and the international community but also between the international community and Chinese dissent, indicating that these celebrities have the potential to grow into all-star diplomats, possessing influence and force. China's recruitment of Hollywood actors to diplomatically lobby on its behalf is not unusual. Acting as the public face for a nation's interest through diplomatic discussions or appearances is dubbed as "celebrity diplomacy". Paradoxically, most of the time, charitable advocacy by celebrity/Hollywood is not seen at the expense of patriotism for the U.S., their own peoples, or their government policies.

Seemingly removed from politics, the high caliber of celebrities can be advertising tools on landscapes of international relations due to their immense impact on consumers all over the world. As a matter of fact, some cultural scholars have ultimately taken up a liking to their role as celebrity advocates of international human rights. Diplomatic areas that stars have a particularly significant effect in, to the class which does not partake in watching news programs dealt with issues they are not accustomed to, are disease, hunger, poverty, refugee flight, racism, and ethnic cleansing. Furthermore, most boulevard scandals, particularly marriage break-ups of celebrity couples, only affect the tabloid press in contrast with celebrities' trips to get to know about events in other countries first-hand. These are international news today.

CHAPTER 6

Ethical Considerations

The study of celebrities is a contested area. Our individual fascination with celebrity icons lives on their capacity to embody tangible star power – an indescribable yet palpable hub of influence, force, and verve. Yet, the desires that celebrities elicit derive from an attribution of star power. The debate of the degree of control that stars have over the tactical construction of their public personae – still, ethical questions remain. After all, those who are the subjects of our associated intrigue are not just pulp fiction characters – they are people: mothers, daughters, sons, siblings, friends, partners, etc. Those who grew up watching Macaulay Culkin probably grow their autobiographical personae hand-in-hand with screen iconography. If you needed a more scholarly elucidation: 'celebrity culture produces a despairing vision of fame, apathetically and antagonistically reached. This symptomatic or key-postmodern dimension of despair used to be largely and effectively repudiated by the genius of charity in Christianity.

Indeed, such aspects are also serviceable in celebrity research. In a particularly crucial way, these issues lead us to an excursus into ethics. The section for discussion at this juncture includes copyright and issues of privacy and the conduct of journalists. Yet, the paparazzi issue bursts this bond of loyalty, just as soap opera magazines give an indiscriminate representation to the private lives of actors and actresses. This is quite interesting (not just in terms of moral relay), as one of the most powerful issues in our ethics today is the pressure to discuss how one might protect the privacy and privacy rights of corporal persons such as states, nations, societies, cultures, and individuals from facile media scrutiny and ill-informed tittle-tattle. This final section offers a bit of insight into this new emergent worry. In some seditious ways, we can also probably view it as the logical consequence of what we are now raising as worries about either applause or critique of icons not being sufficiently deep.

Privacy and Paparazzi

The star system is increasingly caught between the scales of privacy, the right to privacy, and the paparazzi closure of their private lives. The motivation for this moral estimation is a critical climate that has already been increasingly defined by the criticisms surrounding the acquisition and enrichment of paparazzi who work without permits and continuously surround the lives of popular figures. This distance is created through increasing paparazzi influence and continuous pressure, merging a multitude of documentation and interview recordings published in the press.

Paparazzi strategies and material roots have reached the minds of media consumers and produced an increasing media concern through a constant siege. This siege affects not only press photographers but also film and television program directors.

In summation, paparazzi policy is worthy of our moral attention. This attention is needed not only against the ideological voyeuristic impetus that amplifies a proliferation of screens and tabloids, but also for critical reflection. The life of a public person essentially ends, as they cannot be enclosed in external images and also be appropriated. The constant attention of the photographers influences the loss of self and the need to expire between adaptation and self-improvement, in order to not lose oneself. As a result, celebrities exploit their life force, like those before them, for their own benefit with the development of the industry and pop culture.

Exploitation of Fame

Illness, misery, and death are sensational and animate the media's "best" (i.e., largest-selling and most-viewed) products. These products flourish in exuberant market economies, which seek ever-greater profits achieved by answering every possible consumer demand. All celebrities, but especially actors and politicians, are exploited by such economies. Actors and politicians all agree to use their prominently visible positions to garner commercial and political favors, respectively. All are "differentiated" markets of talent, playing somewhat different yet closely related roles in the media's consumer and political dramas. Society's self-interested persecutions of its most famous members are represented as a natural extension of attitudes nurtured by gossip, parody, defamation, malice, sadism, fault-identifying, and fault-exaggerating attitudes that we have all accepted.

Much of society also agrees that high-earning actors are likely to be the fortunate and undeserving beneficiaries of good luck, often because they are lucky enough to resemble another contemporary actor or co-star in ways that are only moderately difficult to replicate. Such opinions, it can be hoped, will help keep our exploitative economies representative. Finally, it is emphasized here that the problem with exploitative, sensational stories of the famous is that monetary payment exalts the raw misery suffered by human beings, reducing celebrities even further, to the bottom, as the fully public properties of consumers. Newspapers and other mass media trumpet every malpractice of man and nature, hoping to attract the "eye-balls" of deeply interested and eager consumers to their advertisers.

CHAPTER 7

Gender and Diversity in Celebrity Culture

The representation of celebrities in the media—whether they be press, film or television—must be seriously considered in terms of the power relations between authority and citizen. Most coverage can be seen to be reinforcing of the democratic fabric, i.e. celebrity coverage often endorses or debates such themes as 'rights' and 'personal freedom' while using a generalized set of personal lifestyles as a hook for the story. Nonetheless, this sort of reporting can be seen as dangerous if polity is allowed to be based too strongly on the so-called 'personal virtues' of a leader. There exists a large amount of gossipy journalist voyeurism as practiced by the tabloids and entertainment television magazines, and the authors of this present volume see this as reinforcing contemporary celebrity status as negative while representing celebrity consumers as nothing more interested in what 'stars' eat and how big they are.

Moreover, the representation of celebrities has other dynamics to be observed. Gender and ethnicity are often the lens through which celebrity icons are seen. Irish and Polish American celebrities become stand-ins for U.S. capitalist culture, stereotype, oppression, and desire. Derris additionally uses feminism to give a clue as to the changes in celebrity style and star-making. The horizons through which celebrity-making consciousness takes celebrities seriously and values their individual difference, particularly as it pertains to the dissolution of the gender binary. Celebrity-making is as well discussed in light of the transgender.

Representation and Stereotypes

Despite the growing interest in celebrity culture, limited research has attempted to explore the popularity and impact of iconic figures. There are far fewer studies concentrating on on-screen representations of celebrity icons, with hardly any interrogating changes in the portrayal of such individuals, or the impact of being labeled an icon on the celebrity or indeed their audience. Considering the extensive research on the construction and evolution of stars in the stardom literature, this paper sought to address this gap in the field, comparing and contrasting Hollywood actors and musicians. This involved exploring differences between these two groups in terms of gender and race/ethnicity, in addition to analyzing audience appeal and their recent portrayal in both biopics and documentary film. As the fields of on- and offline celebrity have grown, and works on identity and the celebrity brand have increased, looking at some initial ideas about representation and possible stereotypes seemed timely.

This section examines gender and the portrayal of diversity within stardom and suggests some ideas for developing papers in these areas. Famous individuals on stage or on screen often come to personify various groups, so it is useful to develop an understanding of how these hero/heroines are represented, critiqued or parodied. Issues of representation intersect with that of stereotyping. Celebrations of celebrity as icon frequently fix celebrities in normative categories. When thinking of gender, ethnicity, and race, many iconic men and women appear to display a quantifiable hegemony. Concern about the homogeneity of the representations can also be found in a number of journalists' critiques of the 'white-washed' awards shows honoring the icons of country music.

Intersectionality

Since the beginning of popular media's rise to power, the media development scholar Douglas Kellner explained that studies started focusing on the influence it exerts on women, often overlooking the extent to which women are "the other," itself defined in relation to men; and subsequently, black women. This section is (ambitiously) an attempt to address some of the "intersectionality" of celebrity, highlighting the interconnected "critical terminant" effects of gender, sexuality, race. The feminist scholar bell hooks argued that, while male slaveholders could fulfill a voyeuristic fantasy on black female slave bodies, black female slaves were not an object of the same order for white women: "the black men, the black women, and the black children slaves on the auction block were like appliances. When sold or traded to white families in constant search of cheap labor, their primary task would be to meet the labor needs of their new employers. There was a recognition that men and boys would be suited best for heavy labor, while women and girls provided housework or breastfeeding labor, but these racial slaves were not just simply appliances: they also represented a source of female labor in racialized ways".

The ways in which celebrity female visages differ from and align with these significant historical and contemporary intersections of race, sexuality, and class is a significant structural force in plurality cultures, contributing to a postcolonial politics of commodification and distinction with capital and colonialism. Celebrity culture – that is, the public consumption of the private lives of figures such as Princess Diana, or the politicians and popular 'powerbrokers' that now take up increasing space in weekly glossies – might be feminized, but the strategies of survival that female icons employ under the capitalist media demand are activated in an intricate interconnected matrix of veiling and dress, deception and denial. These workings of at-the-movies femininity overlay in unsettlingly complex, and not always finally stratified, ways with visually available race, sexuality or ethnicity. So, different critical race theory approaches are far from aligning with either post-feminism or a Cartesian fantasy of the abolition of gender, which may or may not be bound up with changing sartorial displays and language from the lips of catachresis-prone icons: indeed, they provide critical purchase on intersections of constructed difference and the "complicité (pas de deux [chic])" of active superficial banal chic undressing entrepreneurs in gender, race, sexuality and ethnic media spectacle.

CHAPTER 8

Globalization and Cultural Exchange

The twenty-first century has seen fame attain a global, influential and valuable commodity when thinking about how celebrity is established within entertainment industries. Our focus on Hollywood exporting film stars to other markets is an attempt to explain Hollywood's globally dominant film industry, which arguably emerged as a response to legal blocks on vertically integrated practices in the U.S., and which established an export market through various 'hard' and 'soft' trade barriers (restrictive state trade practices, the major vertically integrated distribution firms exporting to the rest of the world, and the running of foreign distribution companies by American expatriates). Today U.S. trade embargos cover virtually all countries but Canada; the term 'Hollywood' (the blending of 'Hollywood' and 'Bollywood'), coined by the Los Angeles Times, has come to signify a movement of talent between U.S. productions and the Indian film industry.

Celebrities are, of course, exchangeable and, except where contractual agreements protect local territories (see, for instance, the analysis of global-level anti-covenant laws in Section 8), the international community is available to any star who can make it there without violating a trade practices act. It is this cross-cultural adoption of western celebrity that is today dominating the scene; intra-Asian exchanges are marginal when compared with the spread of the Western star across these regions. Bollywood is an exception, and we include sections on east-west star exchanges with India. The audience for this exchange - popular culture and the economy of cinema - is examined in the part of the paper devoted specifically to globalization and cultural exchange.

Hollywood's Influence on Global Cinema

This essay aims to track the direct influence of Hollywood on global cinema through the implementation of hegemonic industry practices. Goals for Hollywood cinema are communicated through celebrity culture and the cloth upon which the archetypal characters and movie stars that once promoted Hollywood's dominion are now printed alongside international icons. Consequently, Tinseltown's famous faces maintain cult popularity with audiences worldwide. This chapter then chronologically elucidates how Hollywood, thereafter the USA, the UK, and Japan have been able to subtly subsume scenarios and character cinema of other non-native industries. Ideological synergy between the socio-political superpower, America, and her extensive imitators is shown to saturate character narratives of global popular cinema.

The advent of narrative cinema in the early 20th century is usually typecast as a period in which the defining norms for classical continuity were still coalescing between national touch-bearers. For Thomas Elsaesser, the content circumscribing a nascent Hollywood was a novel set of enigmatic conventions pertaining to the performance of persona, script, director, narrative, malevolence - a blind system that centered solely on circulation and distribution, production and exhibition, stardom and iconography. Asia-Pacific Imperial interests quickly latched on to this novel system in ensuring they could promote their ambitions on a wider stage: "out of this intense encounter between imperial history, capital consolidation, mass communication, and popular culture, a global Hollywood emerged which did not so much bear the impression of American society and history as help to shape its self-image, interpreting itself for the world and by the descriptions the world furnished in the narratives and fantasies played out in the string of amber-lit moving-image palaces."

Cross-Cultural Celebrity Adoption

The reality of today is that mass-produced images infect the global imagination. This suggests that over the last 20 years, the acceleration of digitization - the spread of high-speed internet and the handset version - has deconstructed the time and space of home-grown fame. The most salient evidence is that the traffic of celebrity images, logos, and other ad-centric representations is gluttonously smuggled across national frontiers. Since 9-11, those charming boys and fragile girls selling Coke and Honda, and Justin Timberlake and Britney Spears, have become increasingly popular in transnational markets. It has been estimated by the Corporate Celebrity Marketing Survey that $20 billion a year was spent on casting stars at the beginning of the 21st century and that, three years and one internet bubble later, 73 percent of budget marketers wanted a Hollywood/ TV celebrity endorsement, down from 86 percent.

It is noted by Len Masterman in his study of the national and transnational character of celebrity profile that despite this preponderance of Hollywood in the acts of celebrity endorsement in the past 30 years, the relationship between the Star-Self and the image reflect traditional cultural values. For that very reason, the present project is designed to pick up where Masterman left off, to turn the gaze in the opposite direction, across international boundaries, for a glimpse of reception and adaptation at the receiving end. What happens when Hollywood acts to project American images beyond Yankee shores? What mix of selective reception and creative remembering emerges when stars, images, and tales cross cultural borders?

CHAPTER 9

The Dark Side of Fame

Celebrities are idolized around the world, with millions wanting to know, look like, or live like them. But there is a distinct dark side to this kind of international praise, i.e., superstars constantly live under the scrutiny of those who admire and judge them. Unfortunately, the downsides of celebrating icons can take tragic proportions. For instance, Chrissy Teigen revealed in a string of tweets that famous men and women reading and believing in the mirage of online beauty can become obsessed with maintaining appearances to conceal hardships. Stars, too, endure tragedies and setbacks, and the pressure not to show these struggles can often push them over the edge. Although fans continue to speculate, the fates of Marilyn Monroe, Princess Diana, Kurt Cobain, Heath Ledger, and Whitney Houston, among many others, demonstrate a crucial point: fame is not always as it seems. Consequently, it's our duty to acknowledge the outliers who are submerged beneath the glamorous film premieres, party nights, and television interviews. Here's a look at the tragic side of becoming a symbol of celebrity.

Substance abuse, mental health crises, felonies, and infidelities are the usual triggers of movie star fascination or refrain, what would prompt irrational actions by gawkers and media likers to get the dirt or the news on a scandal, causing the celeb to fall or to soar.

The viciously hungry press has outshone itself on multiple occurrences. Years of public battling is the result of substance addiction and similar Hollywood answers. Celebs also abuse food to control them or ease their steady tension in their regular lives. Chrissy, the more brutal British government, has recognized her poorer self as a struggle sponsor, nominated for work on behalf of assistance and feeding women in Liberia. Abbey inspire is in the prime of her influence, appearing in publications and recently marrying and having kids. However, they have suffered audaciously from crippling disease, which is one of the worst psychosomatic disorders prevailing in a celeb human. Gary is a courageous TV host and cookery writer managing agoraphobic with therapy. In response, she recently issued a letter to fans describing her dispute with the change in hopes that they will better understand her recent behaviour. Tegan pop star Sinead O'Connor had a number of best singles, including "Nothing Compares 2 U" and appeared in the fairiest films of Ireland. In recent years, the stubborn numbers have been highly effective, widely condemned and advocated for her cloistering as a mentally ill soul. In finality, what counts is that all things considered, superstars such as these are sensationalized and even annihilated for living with and owning their human flaws. More disturbing are the surge of young idealising fans who conclude similiar self loath. The truth is that being born with you as the commodity is insufferable.

Substance Abuse and Mental Health

Media icons are often the idols and envy of audiences; however, this is an incomplete portrayal. Increasingly, celebrities have begun using their platforms to champion mental health awareness as they try to cope with the aforementioned exposure and succeed at promoting healthier lifestyles to others. Alcohol and other drug abuse is undeniably high among celebrities in already-daunting industries like music and film. Intensely stressful schedules, unpreventable publicity, the need to adapt to an ever-evolving public persona, the potential for brilliant ideas to plunge unexpectedly, and the enormous pressure of staying relevant continue to take a toll on many stars. This only addresses a few issues contributing to the difficulties faced not only by celebrities but by anyone in the public eye.

What is often overlooked is the effect of being viewed by millions and needing to constantly present a drastically conditioned persona to the fans waiting to hear from you. Dissociating from an individual's true self after being exposed to unexpectedly overwhelming public feedback is not uncommon. Fame can provide such a sudden divergence in an individual's identity, lifestyle, and entire world. Celebrity also leads to unique forms of stress resulting from time needed for travel, autographs, appearances, time handling, phone calls, and working rather than living for most of the year. The tactics employed by stars, including the option to constantly be surrounded by a few friendly faces (posse), sometimes stunt their engagement efforts to maximize their entire career and grow their small range of close friends. Celebrity status also allows hires to run the length of their careers not without the potential for attachment of potential fans facing a pictureless reality that could be anything they want.

Scandals and Controversies

One recurring motif in the biographies and news about celebrity icons - irrespective of industry or field of accomplishment - is the observation that they are regularly followed by scandals, unethical discourses, or anything that deviates from "a post-it love" world. A sticky narrative tape surrounds public figures. As Reese et al. describe for an analysis of 106 media reports about the 2015 FIFA corruption scandal, these controversies are typically presented as iconic deviations from the norm and consumed for their capacity as a scandal due to the cutting of norms and rules. Indeed, the word "scandal" implies that a subject becomes a story that becomes a bad story. Flowing from historical roots in the "broken body," a scandal, referenced for example in the New Testament, is not an offense, but the event of an offense. That you can be not content with someone is one thing, but that you find it scandalous, drawing a growling society together, is another. Thus, a special "power of the negative" is found in scandalization, which offers a specular negativity of the world to us. As a Deleuzian event of identity, the scandal can dethrone a king and create the subject of a story. The iconographer creates the model; the scandal creates the story. The two dance in clear tension.

Scandals are usually considered through the ethics of coverage, but it is equally possible to consider the ethics of interest. Why is failing or wrongdoing, why is infidelity, and finally decline so appealing, and how is a life's work ever to be cleaned if culture returns irreversibly to a dolorous circle? Let us hesitantly suggest that there is something of value in the step back from following every twist in the life of a beautiful person. When "texts become thin," when "shame dissipates or negates information's cognitive demands" in the "strangling narrative," we all stop the possibility of demanding excellence from a tale that tells us more about ourselves than about a skewed life lived off-center.

CHAPTER 10

The Future of Celebrity Icons

Where will the world be in 50 years in terms of celebrity power and influence? The chapter authors generally agree that celebrities will continue to be powerful but are uncertain who they might be. They do expect increasing generational disparities in celebrity interest, with older generations likely continuing to have celebrities from days past become icons while younger people may have less of an attachment to then-current and future celebrities due to increased access to success and pop culture exposure. The potential for backlash against celebrities perceived to be "overexposed" is considered to be a potential problem for the cult of celebrity, as fans may eventually grow tired of constant exposure and clamor for more flesh than hype. The most effective celebrities of the future must strive to be known and "liked" (liking them is important to offset the potentially greater test for negative publicity and to be able to match their fans in a conversation, not just a monologue). The entire landscape could collapse for the J. Loves and J. Beanz of the world as the public is increasingly exposed to people who could no longer hide their issues of behavior and character.

The longevity of corporate versus celebrity influence is likely to vary greatly depending on the type of product the endorser is associated with, with publications and guidance labeled celebrities most likely to be unsuccessful on the merit or demerit of the products they represent. A tendency to be shorter for "convenience" commodities (those that do not need to be experienced) and generally less trusted or endorsed. As public sympathy norms shift from those that are pure and rational to those that increase and magnify the "sloppiness" of everyday "issues" that affect success, models and willing to be seen. This can expose some to be less than advertised, like little celebrity wizards with dubious charms. Celebrity agents can extend the fame of today's cyberstars by aggressively managing relationships in an intermedia environment.

Emerging Trends

Emerging research on celebrity culture highlights the unique influences of individual celebrities in today's society. Given the rapid commercialization of new media, the development of computer graphics and celebrities, the impact of celebrities can certainly be expected to increase. From this perspective, the power of iconic celebrities will evolve in multiple directions in the future, as possible nonlinear trends demonstrate: Pervasive celebrity influence. With digital and virtual technologies continuing to advance, as part of the usual daily media consumption repertoire of billions of people around the world, social media interactions with celebrities will likely become as widespread and ubiquitous as email and internet use by most human beings.

Chiou and Chang (2015) also note that recent increases in social media usage and in the use of tactically enacted "hundreds of million dollar business campaigns" are contributing to the growth of parasocial relationships with sports stars, even replacing face-to-face relationships for some fans. Moreover, people who go on to become "famous and talented" have always been revered and respected. Some consumers and fans admire the skill and achievement levels of recognized experts and elite performers in music, sports, movies, and other arts and entertainment. Fans of these cultural activities may want to learn a skill they admire from or with someone who has demonstrated these abilities and possibilities, and these experts and pros may become celebrities (Molloy et al., 2018).

Sustainability and Longevity

A considerable amount of time and resources tend to be invested in creating and revitalizing icons who are expected to carry the stories of cultural representative interpretation and meaning over time, particularly across epochs and subcultures. After establishing such celebrity status, the next stage, and continuing challenge, is in sustaining and negotiating the shifts and repositionings that enable the figure to endure as "culturally significant". The construction of such would be difficult to pin down and quantify, but could include a combination of the number of different routes already mentioned that the celebrity has, in the first instance, become iconic. All of which allow the conferral of personal qualities such as uniqueness and exceptionality which underline their statistically abnormal accretion of cultural capital, as well as more strategic aids to consumability found in adaptation to audience desires and the wider commercial context. Helping establish their very celebrity/stardom initially would also permit symptoms (almost the pathological personal syndrome or propensity towards addiction and excesses) for the stars to reinvigorate their image and impact in a wider context.

Various mechanisms allow a period to pass but for the individual (or at least the iconic representation of them) to appear undiminished by this process. The hallmarks of the celebrity culture discussed above (such as quality of accessibility and the texts as so intensely "lived" by the person they are attributed to that other neighboring or interspersed texts and beliefs cannot compete with it) might simply be reinvoked (and indeed as demonstrated in Aitliffe & Jancovich, June 2005, are also constantly renegotiable). A recent example of this is with Kurt Cobain and the qualifications process that has accompanied the passing of each year of the date of his suicide. Celebrity culture has been most vocal in expressing a belief in accessibility, and even in expressing an accessibility of the article of death. This, as the Coroners inquest showed, is a mythical accessibility as we are invited only to "participate" metaphorically, principally as consumers and just as importantly not to have participated in the consumption (making one in a selective state of denial). Furthermore, we do not apparently have the right to that participation and interrogation of the celebrities' expertise in the subject of the article of death is a necessary condition for meaningful participation. These myths stand as convenient qualities when sustaining the impact of that loss year on year for fans, audience, and media in a celebrity-led (if that is the appropriated term) death industry.